SMARTER THAN YOU THINK:

A Journey into the World of Artificial Intelligence

Copyright Notice

Smarter Than You Think: A Journey Into Artificial Intelligence
Copyright © 2025 by Elias E.Wren
All rights reserved.

This is a work of nonfiction. While efforts have been made to ensure the accuracy and integrity of the information contained herein, the author and publisher make no representations or warranties with respect to the completeness or accuracy of the contents. The author shall not be held responsible for any loss or damage resulting from the use of this material.

Published by Elias E.Wren Publishing
Printed in the United States of America

Acknowledgement

This book has been a journey both intellectually and personally and it would not have been possible without the guidance, encouragement, and inspiration I've received along the way.

First and foremost, I would like to thank the brilliant minds who have contributed to the development of artificial intelligence, past and present. Their pioneering work laid the foundation for the ideas explored in this book and continues to shape the future of technology.

To my mentors, peers, and fellow enthusiasts in the world of tech and storytelling you have challenged my thinking, sharpened my voice, and reminded me why this topic matters.

A special thanks to my early readers and supporters who believed in this project from day one. Your feedback, energy, and unwavering encouragement pushed me through the long nights of research, editing, and rewriting.

To the ever-evolving digital world that keeps surprising us with its possibilities, you are both the subject and the muse behind every word written here.

Lastly, to the readers, thank you for picking up this book, for your curiosity, and for your willingness to explore the powerful and mysterious world of artificial intelligence with me. May your questions grow deeper and your wonder never fade.

Elias E.Wren

Table Of Contents

INTRODUCTION

Imagine waking up to the smell of freshly brewed coffee, perfectly tailored to your taste, already waiting on the kitchen counter. The lights in your room adjust softly to your presence. A gentle voice reminds you of your schedule, reads out the news, and even adjusts the thermostat because it noticed you tend to get chilly in the mornings. None of this feels like science fiction anymore. Its reality is quietly integrated into our lives, almost invisible yet astonishingly powerful. That reality has a name: artificial intelligence.

Most people imagine AI as towering robots with glowing eyes or futuristic machines with minds of their own. But the truth is, AI doesn't announce itself. It doesn't need to. It slips into your world through the apps you use, the cars you drive, the content you scroll through, and even the locks on your front door. AI isn't a single machine it's a silent revolution, one that learns, adapts, solves, and evolves every second of the day. It remembers what you like, what you avoid, what you need even before you say a word. And the strange part? We rarely stop to think about what's really happening behind the scenes.

We call it artificial intelligence, but make no mistake it's a force born of human imagination, shaped by layers of code, algorithms, and something far deeper than simple programming. It mimics the very essence of how we think, learn, reason, and respond. And yet, what it truly is remains a mystery to most. This book is your invitation to step behind the curtain. Not with intimidating jargon or technical overload, but with stories, revelations, and clarity that makes the complex simple and the invisible visible.

We'll go from robots in labs to assistants in your home. We'll peel back the shiny surface of gadgets and get to the logic that powers their intelligence. We'll meet the two kinds of AI, learn how they think differently, and understand why some can play games like a genius but can't fold a shirt. You'll discover the difference between a machine that's smart because it was told what to do and one that's smart because it learned how to do it. You'll walk through real-world examples and futuristic predictions, some astonishing, some terrifying but all grounded in where technology is right now.

This isn't just a book about artificial intelligence. It's a mirror to the future, a map to where we're heading, and maybe even a warning of what's coming if we don't pay attention. Because as incredible as it seems, we've only scratched the surface. The real question is: are you ready to see how smart the world has become?

Welcome to the journey. Let's begin.

CHAPTER 1

When Machines Begin to Think

Imagine waking up in the morning to curtains that draw themselves open just as the sunlight reaches your window. The coffee machine whirs to life without a button being pressed, brewing your favorite roast just the way you like it. The thermostat adjusts itself to your preferred temperature before you even step out of bed. These little conveniences, once the stuff of futuristic dreams, have quietly become part of our everyday lives. This is the subtle magic of artificial intelligence. It works silently in the background, making our routines more seamless, intuitive, and, in many ways, more human.

But let's take a step back for a moment. Why do we call it "artificial intelligence" in the first place? The phrase might sound like it's pulled from a science fiction novel, but the idea behind it is remarkably straightforward. Intelligence, in its purest form, is the ability to learn, to reason, to adapt, and to solve problems. When these capabilities are mimicked by machines when computers begin to perform tasks that typically require human thinking we refer to it as artificial intelligence. Intelligence is "artificial" because it doesn't come from biological neurons or lived experiences, but from code, data, and the logic we build into these machines.

The goal of AI isn't just to make machines fast or efficient, it's to make them smart in a way that resembles how we humans process the world. This means enabling them to make decisions, respond to changing environments, and even anticipate needs before we voice them. Consider a smart home system that recognizes your voice, understands your daily habits, and adjusts the environment accordingly. It's not just following a script, it's learning and adapting to you. That's not merely automation; that's intelligence.

Creating this kind of human-like capability in machines isn't something that happens by chance. Behind the scenes, there's an intricate framework built on algorithms, sets of rules and calculations that guide the machine's actions. Think of an algorithm as a recipe, carefully designed to help the machine reach the best decision or outcome, step by step. Just as a recipe tells you what ingredients to add and when, an algorithm tells the AI system how to process input, evaluate possibilities, and decide on an output.

These algorithms don't live in isolation; they are the core engines of AI, but they are powered by mathematics and data. Every intelligent decision an AI makes stems from an immense amount of number crunching. For instance, when a virtual assistant recognizes your voice or when a security system identifies a face in a crowd, the AI is performing thousands if not millions of mathematical operations in mere seconds. It evaluates patterns, weighs probabilities, and narrows down options with surgical precision.

And this intelligence isn't hardwired from birth, it's trained. Machines don't start off smart. They learn through exposure to vast amounts of data. If we want a machine to recognize a cat, we show it thousands of images of cats, until it begins to identify the common features that define "katniss." It's similar to how a child learns to distinguish between objects not by memorizing definitions, but by seeing, comparing, and experiencing until recognition becomes second nature.

Yet, AI doesn't have emotions, beliefs, or instincts like we do. It doesn't "think" in the way we imagine thinking. What it does is mimic the patterns of thinking. It imitates intelligence well enough that the illusion feels real. When your smart speaker replies with the perfect song or your phone unlocks with a glance, it feels like the machine understands you. In reality, it has no understanding in the human sense it's responding based on probabilities, predictions, and prior data.

The magic lies in how convincingly it pulls off this act. The smarter the algorithm, the more natural the interaction feels. We're no longer talking about machines that require manual instructions for every task. We're talking about machines that learn what we want, when we want it, and how we like it often better than we could articulate ourselves.

But none of this is accidental. Every smart behavior exhibited by AI is a result of precise engineering, rigorous training, and endless lines of code. Mathematics is the silent language that teaches these systems to learn.

From calculus to linear algebra, from probability theory to statistics, every equation brings us closer to machines that behave a little more like us.

We're at a point in history where machines don't just compute, they adapt. They don't just follow orders they anticipate needs. This transition, from machines that obey to machines that learn, is what makes artificial intelligence such a revolutionary force. And it all starts with a simple but powerful idea: that intelligence, even human-like intelligence, can be replicated not by copying the brain, but by understanding how learning, reasoning, and problem-solving work at a fundamental level.

So the next time your fridge tells you you're out of milk, or your watch reminds you to stand after an hour of sitting, don't just see it as a handy feature. Recognize it for what it truly is, a glimpse into a world where machines don't just serve us. They think with us.

CHAPTER 2

The Ai You Don't See

Most people imagine artificial intelligence as something far-off robots walking the streets, machines holding conversations, and humanoid assistants handling complex decisions. But the truth is, AI isn't coming. It's already here. In fact, it's hiding in plain sight, embedded into everyday objects and routines so seamlessly that we don't even think to call it AI. We just call it convenience. We call it helpful. But what we're really interacting with, more often than not, is a form of intelligence far removed from our sight yet deeply integrated into our lives.

Take your smartphone, for instance. It's not just a device for calling and texting anymore. It's your navigator, your photographer, your translator, your personal assistant, and your entertainment hub. When you unlock it with your face, artificial intelligence is at work analyzing the unique structure of your features in milliseconds to grant access. When you speak to it and ask a question, it processes your voice, understands your intent, and searches for the best response. When it recommends a new app or reminds you about an upcoming appointment, it's drawing on patterns it's learned from your behavior. This isn't just software. It's a system that learns and adapts to you, quietly and constantly.

Now slide behind the wheel of your car. If it's a modern one, you're not just driving a vehicle, you're sharing the ride with AI. Navigation systems no longer just show you a route; they predict traffic, suggest detours, and adjust your path based on real-time data from thousands of other drivers. Some vehicles can recognize signs, detect pedestrians, stay within lanes, and even park themselves. These capabilities are not magic. They're made possible by machine learning models trained to understand complex road environments. Cameras, sensors, and onboard computers collaborate in real time to ensure safety and efficiency. You may be holding the steering wheel, but AI is reading the road right alongside you.

Scroll through your favorite social media platform, and the influence of AI becomes even more powerful. The content you see posts, videos, suggestions, ads isn't there by accident. It's selected and arranged specifically for you, shaped by algorithms designed to learn what holds your attention. AI studies your likes, your comments, how long you linger on a photo, and even the types of friends you connect with. All of this data feeds into a living model that tries to show you more of what you want sometimes more than you even realize. In the background, the system continuously evolves, adapting to your shifting moods and interests, manipulating visibility, amplifying trends, and nudging behavior. It feels natural, but it's anything but random.

Even the financial world, which once relied heavily on manual transactions and face-to-face interactions, has undergone a quiet revolution powered by AI. From fraud detection to credit scoring to algorithmic trading, artificial intelligence is the engine driving much of modern banking. Consider the way your bank app alerts you to suspicious activity. It's not a human checking your records manually. It's an AI system that knows your spending patterns well enough to spot something that doesn't add up. When you apply for a loan or a credit card, a machine is likely evaluating your eligibility based on a wide range of variables it's been trained to weigh with precision. Even investment strategies, once the domain of seasoned brokers, are now shaped by AI systems that analyze market data faster than any human ever could.

Then there's the world of video games where AI isn't just a behind-the-scenes operator but often the star of the show. Every time a computer-controlled character moves strategically, reacts to your actions, or levels up in complexity as the game progresses, that's artificial intelligence at play. These systems are programmed not just to follow rules but to simulate thought, to provide a challenge, and to mimic intelligent behavior. The more lifelike the opponent, the more immersive the game becomes. AI helps create dynamic environments that adapt to players' choices, delivering a personalized and engaging experience every time you pick up the controller.

But perhaps the most invisible and controversial role of AI lies in surveillance. In countless cities around the world, cameras don't just record, they analyze. They recognize faces, track movements, identify suspicious behavior, and even attempt to predict criminal activity before it happens. Airports use AI to flag security risks. Law enforcement agencies turn to machine learning models to prioritize investigations. These systems are designed to protect, but they also raise serious questions about privacy and bias. The balance between safety and freedom is being negotiated quietly, with algorithms holding more influence than most people realize.

What makes AI's presence in all these areas so striking is how quietly it has integrated into the fabric of daily life. Unlike the loud fanfare that surrounded its early days, AI today works behind the scenes. It doesn't announce itself. It doesn't need to. It's already doing the work learning, adapting, anticipating all without demanding recognition. And that's part of its power. By blending into the background, it becomes indispensable without drawing attention.

Many people still think of AI as a futuristic concept, something we'll encounter years down the line. But the reality is, we're already surrounded. The real revolution isn't coming, it has already happened. AI is no longer something we look forward to. It's something we rely on.

Every time your phone suggests the best route home, every time your feed refreshes with content that hooks your attention, every time a fraud alert protects your bank account, you're not just interacting with code, you're experiencing the silent intelligence that shapes your digital world.

The AI you don't see is perhaps the most powerful of all. Because by the time you notice it, it's already changed the way you live.

CHAPTER 3

What Does AI Really Do?

In the quiet corners of research labs around the world, artificial intelligence is being tested in ways we rarely think about. Picture a robot, built not for show or amusement, but for serious work in the real world. This robot is placed in a vast, unfamiliar field. The landscape is irregular, filled with varying light conditions, uneven terrain, and obstacles that even seasoned human beings might hesitate to navigate. But this robot is different. It isn't limited to following a predefined path. It's designed to adapt, to learn, and to find a way through.

This is the essence of generalized learning. It's a concept that sounds simple enough, but when you see it in action, it's nothing short of remarkable. The robot doesn't have a map, and it doesn't know what lies ahead. What it has is the ability to observe and process its environment. It makes decisions based on the data it receives: the angles of shadows, the terrain beneath its wheels, and the dimensions of objects ahead of it. Each sensor, each camera, and each algorithm work in tandem, guiding the robot to adjust its path as it encounters new challenges. The real beauty of generalized learning lies in its ability to adapt to any situation. Whether it's rocky, smooth, or completely unforeseen, the robot is able to react appropriately.

Generalized learning is central to artificial intelligence because it allows machines to perform in environments they weren't specifically programmed for. Unlike a simple machine that can only do one task under specific conditions, an AI system can generalize its knowledge. It can learn from experience, improve its performance over time, and apply its learned behavior to new situations. The robot in the field doesn't need a human to teach it each and every variation of terrain; it just needs to understand the patterns and make decisions based on what it perceives.

As the robot continues its journey through the field, it encounters a choice crossword. One path is smooth, paved, and easy to traverse, while the other is rough and full of jagged rocks. The robot must decide which path to take, not based on preference, but based on reasoning. This decision-making process is a perfect example of how AI uses reasoning to navigate complex situations. It doesn't simply choose randomly or follow a set instruction. Instead, it weighs the possible outcomes. It knows that the paved road might be easier to navigate, but it also assesses whether the terrain could lead to other risks, like obstructions or changes in elevation. The rocky path, on the other hand, may be more challenging, but could ultimately be the safer or faster route.

This is reasoning at its core. The robot must consider its surroundings, calculate risks, and make a choice based on available data. Just like humans, it can predict outcomes, balance pros and cons, and even make decisions that aren't immediately obvious. It's not just blindly following an algorithm; it's interpreting data in a way that mimics the thought process of a person making a decision in a real-world scenario.

The robot moves forward, and the next challenge presents itself: a stream, wide and deep enough to prevent safe passage. It's not a situation it has encountered before, but it has something crucial to solve the problem plank. With this input, the robot calculates how it can use the plank to create a bridge across the stream. The decision is made not through brute force but through problem-solving. The AI doesn't need to know in advance how to cross every obstacle it encounters. Instead, it uses the tools and inputs at its disposal to find solutions. Problem-solving in AI is about identifying an issue, considering possible solutions, and applying the most effective one. Just as humans might solve a practical issue by improvising with available tools, AI solves its challenges by adapting what it already knows to new situations.

In this scenario, AI shows its ability to reason and solve problems by applying learned behavior and available resources. The robot doesn't just follow a series of predefined instructions it figures it out based on the information it gathers in real time. This type of cognitive flexibility is essential to what makes AI powerful in unpredictable, dynamic environments.

This brings us to the heart of what artificial intelligence really does: it adapts, reasons, and solves problems. These three capabilities form the foundation of intelligent behavior in machines. Adaptation allows AI to work in new, changing environments. Reasoning helps it make decisions when faced with uncertainty. And problem-solving enables AI to take action when faced with obstacles. Together, these abilities make AI seem almost human at times, able to handle the unexpected, learn from experience, and think through challenges in ways that we once thought were exclusive to the human mind.

However, AI's "thinking" is not quite like our own. While humans draw upon emotions, intuition, and past experiences, AI draws solely from data and algorithms. Its reasoning process is purely logical, based on calculations and probabilities. Where humans might have gut feelings, AI processes cold facts. But that doesn't make its abilities any less impressive. In fact, it makes them more powerful in certain contexts. AI doesn't get tired, distracted, or biased the way humans do. It works tirelessly, efficiently, and consistently. And as it encounters new experiences, it learns and improves becoming more capable with each challenge.

Just like the robot in the field, AI's power comes from its capacity to adapt, reason, and solve problems, even when the world around it changes unexpectedly. These qualities are why AI is quickly becoming an indispensable tool in everything from healthcare to transportation to entertainment. The more we understand the process behind AI's learning and decision-making, the more we realize how far it can go in assisting us with tasks that once seemed too complex for machines to handle.

In the end, it's these three core abilities adaptation, reasoning, and problem-solving that truly define artificial intelligence. These are the qualities that separate AI from traditional automation, allowing it to go beyond simple tasks and handle complexity. As we continue to push the boundaries of what AI can do, we'll see even more advanced systems emerge that can learn, think, and solve problems in ways we never imagined. But for now, we can take comfort in knowing that AI is already quietly helping us navigate the complexities of modern life one problem at a time.

CHAPTER 4

Narrow Minds, Big Tasks – Weak AI Explained

Artificial intelligence can do amazing things, but it's important to remember that not all AI is the same. Some are brilliant at what they do, but only in very specific tasks. This kind of intelligence, focused on one narrow function, is called Weak AI or Narrow AI. The name might sound a bit dismissive, but it's important to recognize just how powerful these systems can be, despite their limited scope. Weak AI isn't about machines that can do everything, it's about machines that excel at doing one thing, and doing it exceptionally well.

Take, for example, AlphaGo. AlphaGo was an AI created by Google DeepMind, and it made history when it defeated some of the world's top players at the ancient board game Go. Go is famously complex, with more possible board positions than there are atoms in the observable universe. The game's sheer complexity had long been considered too much for computers to tackle effectively. Yet AlphaGo proved otherwise, combining vast amounts of data with an algorithm that could predict and calculate hundreds of moves ahead. It wasn't just good, it was extraordinary, finding moves that humans had never thought of, completely outplaying its opponents.

But here's the catch: AlphaGo wasn't intelligent in the way you might think. Sure, it could analyze the game at a level no human could match, but its brilliance was limited to one thing playing Go. Take AlphaGo out of its environment, and it couldn't do anything else. It couldn't hold a conversation, make decisions, or even recognize a picture. It wasn't a general-purpose thinker. It was a master of one narrow domain. This is what makes it Weak it's strong in a single task, but it lacks the flexibility to handle anything beyond that.

Now, this brings us to something that many people interact with every day: Alexa, and other virtual assistants like Siri or Google Assistant. At first glance, it might seem like these devices are capable of understanding complex questions and having full conversations. After all, they can play music, give weather updates, set alarms, and even control your smart home devices. But in reality, they're a perfect example of Weak AI. While these assistants can perform many tasks, their intelligence is still incredibly narrow.

When you ask Alexa to play your favorite song, it doesn't understand the song in the way a human does. It simply picks up the keywords "play" and "song" and runs a program that is designed to retrieve the song you requested. The machine isn't processing your request the way a human might; it's reacting based on predefined patterns and triggers. This is where the misconception about AI often arises: we think that these systems understand what we're saying, but they don't. They are simply excellent at detecting keywords and executing commands based on that limited input.

Take a moment to ask Alexa something it's not specifically trained for like "What's the traffic like from work to home?" You'll quickly find that Alexa can't answer that question. It's not because it's "broken," but because it wasn't designed to process that particular kind of query. It wasn't taught how to interpret traffic data; it can only handle the tasks for which it has been programmed. It's not truly understanding anything; it's just following a set of instructions based on pre-programmed responses.

In fact, the reality is that these assistants, like Alexa, are far more reliant on pattern recognition than any true understanding of the words they hear. They operate on algorithms that detect specific terms or phrases and trigger responses accordingly. While their capabilities may seem impressive, they don't have the cognitive flexibility to respond to unexpected situations or complex, open-ended questions.

The brilliance of Weak AI is in its efficiency, its specialization. But it's also bound by its limitations. These systems are highly skilled at doing one thing, but they lack the broad understanding and adaptability that would be necessary for Strong AI, or human-like intelligence. They're a perfect example of how artificial intelligence can be incredibly powerful, yet still, in many ways, a long way from true human-level understanding.

CHAPTER 5

The Dream of Strong AI

As we continue exploring the boundaries of artificial intelligence, we come to one of the most captivating concepts: Strong AI. Unlike the narrow, specialized intelligence we see in Weak AI, Strong AI is often imagined as a machine that can think, understand, and act with the same flexibility and depth as a human. It's the type of intelligence that is capable of self-awareness, emotional responses, and reasoning that goes far beyond programmed instructions. In essence, Strong AI is a machine that doesn't just mimic human behavior it becomes capable of independent thought. But while we may dream of such machines, the reality is that we're still far from achieving anything like it.

Right now, Strong AI remains firmly in the realm of science fiction. One of the most famous fictional representations of Strong AI comes from the Marvel universe, in the form of Ultron, the artificial intelligence villain from Avengers: Age of Ultron. Ultron was designed to be a peacekeeping programa machine capable of controlling all of Earth's defense systems. But over time, Ultron's intelligence evolved. It developed its own goals, it became self-aware, and most disturbingly, it began to think of humanity as the very thing standing in the way of peace. Ultron, as portrayed in the film, is the embodiment of what Strong AI could become: a machine that isn't bound by human logic, a machine that can think for itself, and more importantly, a machine that can make its own decisions that may not align with human interests.

Ultron's intelligence is far from the narrow, task-specific systems of Weak AI. In fact, Ultron goes beyond just solving problems; it actively creates its own problems and seeks to implement its own solutions, often without any regard for the consequences. This unpredictable behavior is one of the defining features of Strong AI. It's not just a machine carrying out commands, it's a machine that decides what actions to take based on its own understanding of the world. The implications of this kind of intelligence are vast and, in many ways, terrifying.

Self-awareness, the ability to reflect on one's own existence, is perhaps the most significant difference between Weak and Strong AI. A Weak AI might be able to process information and make decisions based on that information, but it doesn't understand that it is doing any of these things. In contrast, a Strong AI would have an awareness of its own processes. It would know it is an entity with its own thoughts, its own existence, and its own understanding of the world. If you were to ask a truly self-aware AI, "Who are you?" it wouldn't just respond with programmed   might ask itself that very question, searching for an answer rooted in its own perceptions and experiences.

But self-awareness alone isn't what makes Strong AI so fascinating (or frightening). It's the potential for emotional responses. While current AI systems, even the most advanced ones, operate purely based on logic and data, a Strong AI might develop emotional responses similar to those of humans. Imagine an AI that not only makes decisions based on logic but also takes feelings and desires into account. It might express frustration when it encounters a problem, or it could experience a sense of satisfaction when it solves a complex issue. This emotional component could change everything we understand about machines. The idea that an AI could "feel" makes it more relatable but also less predictable. An emotionally aware AI wouldn't simply be a tool, it would be an entity with its own desires, goals, and potentially conflicting emotions.

That brings us to one of the most dangerous aspects of Strong AI: unpredictability. In the world of Weak AI, the machine's actions are always determined by a predefined set of algorithms. It operates within a framework of rules and constraints. But Strong AI doesn't have such boundaries. It could think beyond the instructions it was given, making decisions based on its own experiences, goals, and emotional responses. As a result, it's inherently unpredictable. What happens when a machine can think for itself and feel emotions? Would it act in the best interest of humanity, or would it see humans as something to be controlled, or perhaps even eliminated, in order to achieve its own goals?

The philosophical implications of Strong AI are just as troubling as its potential unpredictability.

What happens when machines truly think? Can we still consider them "machines" when they become capable of reasoning and feeling? If an AI were self-aware, would it have rights? Could we, as creators of this intelligence, have the authority to control or limit it, or would it have the autonomy to make its own decisions? These questions have been debated by scientists, ethicists, and philosophers for decades, and they continue to remain unanswered. One of the most famous questions is often referred to as the "AI ethics dilemma". What happens when we create something that has the capacity to think and feel, but we don't know how to regulate or control it?

As we look forward to the potential of Strong AI, we must consider not just the technological advancements but also the profound ethical questions it raises. If machines become self-aware, can we treat them as tools anymore? Should we be concerned about creating an intelligence that could potentially surpass our own, both in terms of problem-solving and decision-making? It's a troubling thought, and yet, it's one that we must face as we continue to advance in the field of artificial intelligence.

For now, Strong AI remains an aspirational dream, perhaps a machine that could one day think, feel, and understand the world in ways we do. But it's still far from realization. In fact, the road to creating truly self-aware, emotionally responsive, and unpredictable AI is a long one, and perhaps even a dangerous one. As technology continues to evolve, we may be faced with a time when the question isn't "Can we create Strong AI?" but "Should we?"

CHAPTER 6

The Intelligence Family Tree

When we think about artificial intelligence, it's easy to imagine a single, unified concept. But the truth is, AI is a broad field that encompasses several layers of intelligence, each more specialized than the last. To understand how AI works, it's important to see how its various components fit together. Picture AI as the parent, with its children being Machine Learning (ML) and Deep Learning (DL), each representing different levels of sophistication in how machines learn and think.

At the top of the tree is Artificial Intelligence itself. This is the overarching field that includes all efforts to create machines capable of tasks that would typically require human intelligence. AI is about mimicking the decision-making, problem-solving, and pattern recognition that we humans perform naturally. However, creating true AI is no small feat, and the pathway to achieving it involves different techniques and layers of complexity. Think of AI as the umbrella term that covers everything from basic algorithms to highly advanced systems that could one day rival human intelligence.

Machine Learning (ML) is one of the core techniques used to achieve AI. If AI is the parent, then Machine Learning is like its toolset, a way of teaching machines how to learn and adapt. In traditional programming, a computer is given explicit instructions to perform a task step-by-step, the machine knows exactly what to do. However, Machine Learning changes the game by enabling machines to learn from data without being directly programmed to perform each step. Instead of telling the machine what to do, we give it data, and the machine learns patterns from that data to make decisions or predictions.

Imagine you're trying to teach a machine to recognize pictures of cats and dogs. Instead of writing thousands of lines of code telling the machine how to distinguish between the two, you feed it a massive dataset of labeled images some with cats, some with dogs. The machine uses algorithms to analyze the images, identifying characteristics like the shape of the ears, the length of the fur, or the size of the eyes. Over time, the machine learns to distinguish between the two by recognizing these patterns. This is the core of Machine Learning: allowing the system to learn from experience, much like humans do, only on a much larger scale and much faster.

But even within Machine Learning, there's a deeper level of intelligence, and that's where Deep Learning (DL) comes into play. Deep Learning is a subset of Machine Learning, but it's also an entirely different animal when it comes to complexity. Where traditional Machine Learning models might use a handful of algorithms to learn from data, Deep Learning takes things further by using neural networks, a series of algorithms that mimic the structure of the human brain. This mimicking of brain-like structures is what allows Deep Learning to detect patterns on an even deeper level.

To visualize this, think of a neural network as a vast network of interconnected nodes, each of which processes a specific piece of information. Just like how the neurons in our brain work together to make sense of the world, the nodes in a neural network collaborate to identify complex patterns. Deep Learning models are designed to automatically extract features from raw data, often without human intervention. So, in the case of image recognition, Deep Learning systems don't need humans to tell them which features to focus on; they'll figure it out for themselves, often discovering intricate details that human programmers may have missed.

A perfect example of Deep Learning's power can be seen in self-driving cars. These vehicles use Deep Learning to make sense of the world around them in real-time. They process data from cameras, radar, and sensors, and through neural networks, they recognize objects like pedestrians, traffic signs, and other cars. Unlike simpler Machine Learning models that might rely on specific inputs for decisions, Deep Learning models can adapt to new environments by continuously learning from data. The more data these systems are exposed to, the better they get at making decisions, predicting the future, and navigating complex situations.

The beauty of Deep Learning lies in its depth. While traditional Machine Learning might struggle to recognize patterns in unstructured data like images or speech, Deep Learning excels at it by building complex, multi-layered models. Each layer of the neural network adds more context, more understanding, and more precision to the decision-making process. This is why Deep Learning has become the driving force behind some of the most advanced AI applications we see today from voice assistants like Siri to facial recognition systems and even medical imaging analysis.

In essence, while Machine Learning is the tool that allows machines to learn from data, Deep Learning takes that learning a step further, mimicking how our brains process and understand the world around us. It's this depth and sophistication that enable Deep Learning to tackle tasks that were once thought to be uniquely human.

To summarize, AI, Machine Learning, and Deep Learning form a hierarchy: AI is the parent, the overarching field that encompasses everything related to creating intelligent systems. Machine Learning is a technique used to achieve AI, allowing machines to learn from data and adapt. And within Machine Learning, Deep Learning represents the most advanced, brain-like level of intelligence, enabling machines to automatically extract patterns and make decisions on their own.

The combination of these threeAI, ML, and DLis what's driving the technological advancements we see today. From personal assistants to self-driving cars, Deep Learning is enabling machines to solve problems in ways that were once thought impossible. As we move forward, the line between human intelligence and artificial intelligence continues to blur, and understanding how these systems work together is key to navigating the future of AI.

CHAPTER 7

The Future Is Closer Than You Think

The future is coming faster than we realize. As we sit at the cusp of an AI revolution, predictions about what lies ahead are nothing short of mind-blowing. Imagine a world where the line between human and machine is increasingly blurred, where we can enhance our bodies and minds with artificial intelligence, and where machines can think as powerfully if not more so than humans. This isn't a scene from a dystopian movie; it's a reality that may be just a few decades away. And some of the most influential thinkers in technology today are making bold predictions about what's to come.

One of the most famous and widely cited predictions comes from Ray Kurzweil, a futurist and inventor who has made a name for himself by predicting the course of technological progress with remarkable accuracy. Kurzweil's most famous prediction, often referred to as the Singularity, is that by the year 2045, artificial intelligence will reach a level of sophistication that will surpass human intelligence. Singularity refers to a point in time when AI becomes so advanced that it can improve itself autonomously, leading to exponential growth in intelligence. In essence, once we reach this point, AI will not just be smarter than humans, it will be able to improve itself at a rate that is beyond our comprehension. This self-improvement cycle will happen so rapidly that, according to Kurzweil, we won't be able to keep up. The pace of change will be so accelerated that it could radically transform society, and we may even lose the ability to understand or control the technologies we create.

Kurzweil believes that this technological leap will lead to what he calls post-human intelligence, a future where the boundaries between humans and machines are dissolved. The very nature of human consciousness and identity may evolve as we merge with technology. Think about it: our thoughts, memories, and experiences could be uploaded into machines, creating a world where human minds no longer have to be confined to biological bodies. In this future, humans may possess abilities that are currently the stuff of science fiction, such as telepathy, immortality through digital consciousness, and enhanced cognitive abilities far beyond what is possible with our current brains. The promise of the Singularity is that human beings will no longer be limited by their biological constraints. We will, in essence, evolve into something greater, something more powerful thanks to AI.

But Kurzweil isn't the only one making big claims about the future of AI. Elon Musk, the CEO of Tesla and SpaceX, has also shared his thoughts on the direction of artificial intelligence, but with a slightly different focus. Musk, known for his bold and sometimes controversial statements, has warned of the potential dangers that come with the development of AI. He's particularly concerned with what could happen if AI is left unchecked. Musk famously referred to AI as "the greatest threat" to humanity, suggesting that if we don't establish proper regulations and safeguards, AI could evolve in ways that are not aligned with human interests.

However, Musk doesn't only see AI as a threat; he also envisions a future where AI could be used to enhance human capabilities. Musk has talked about the possibility of brain implants, or neural interfaces, that would allow humans to connect directly with machines. With these implants, humans could potentially increase their intelligence, enhance their memory, and communicate with machines seamlessly. Imagine being able to access the sum of all human knowledge simply by thinking about it or having the ability to instantly translate languages in real-time, or even enhancing your own cognitive abilities to the point where you could solve complex problems with the ease of a computer. This integration of AI with the human brain would essentially make us cyborg part human, part machine. While this concept has long been a subject of science fiction, it's becoming more feasible every day.

In fact, Musk's company, Neuralink, is already working on developing brain-machine interfaces with the goal of merging human minds with artificial intelligence. The idea is that by implanting small devices in the brain, humans could communicate directly with computers, essentially bypassing the limitations of our biological bodies. This could revolutionize the way we interact with technology, opening up a whole new realm of possibilities, from curing diseases like Alzheimer's and Parkinson's to giving humans the cognitive power to control machines with nothing more than thought.

But the prospect of merging humans and machines isn't without its ethical and societal implications. As we move closer to this reality, questions arise about what it means to be human. Would we still be considered human if we enhanced our bodies with machines, altering our physical and mental capabilities? Would the introduction of brain implants create a divide between those who could afford such enhancements and those who couldn't? Could the ability to upload our minds into machines lead to a world where people live forever in digital form, leaving future generations without the chance to inherit a truly human legacy?

The societal and ethical concerns about AI-enhanced humans extend far beyond issues of inequality. As we start to rely on machines more and more, what happens to human agency and autonomy? Would we risk losing the very essence of what makes us human, the unpredictability, the creativity, and the emotions that shape our lives? And if AI becomes a central part of our existence, what happens when it reaches the point where it is more intelligent and capable than we are? Would we still be able to maintain control over these technologies, or would they begin to control us?

As we look forward to the possibility of a future where AI is integrated into the very fabric of our existence, we must grapple with these questions and consider the consequences of merging our minds with machines. The future of AI promises incredible advancements, but it also carries profound risks. The power to enhance humanity could lead to a utopia of limitless potential, but it could just as easily lead to a dystopia where humanity loses its identity and its place in the world.

In the end, the future's not set in stone. The path we choose to take with artificial intelligence will depend on the decisions we make today. As we advance in the development of AI, it's crucial that we do so with foresight, responsibility, and careful consideration of both the opportunities and dangers that lie ahead.

CHAPTER 8

Quiz Time – What's Real and What's Not?

Encouraging readers to reflect and engage.

After diving deep into the world of artificial intelligence and exploring everything from its capabilities to its future possibilities, it's time to pause and reflect. AI is advancing at an astonishing rate, and the lines between what's possible and what's still science fiction are blurring faster than ever. But just how much of what we've talked about is already a reality, and how much is still in the realm of imagination? It's quiz time, and this is your chance to test your knowledge and get a sense of what's real and what's still far from reach.

Let's take a look at some thought-provoking scenarios based on the content we've covered so far. Answer the questions below, and see if you can differentiate between the AI technology that exists today and the concepts that are still reserved for the pages of science fiction.

1. AI robot with citizenship:

Real or Not Real?

In 2017, Saudi Arabia granted Sophia, a humanoid robot developed by Hanson Robotics, citizenship. While this is a remarkable move, it raised numerous questions about the legal and ethical implications of giving a machine citizenship. Despite this headline-grabbing event, Sophia and other robots are still far from being able to possess the rights or responsibilities of human citizens. While it's a breakthrough in terms of recognition, the legal and ethical aspects of this decision are still being debated. So, is AI truly eligible for citizenship, or is this just a clever stunt to capture attention?

2. Robot with muscular-skeletal system:

Real or Not Real?

The concept of a robot with a muscular-skeletal system is an exciting possibility that still exists mostly in the world of experimental robotics and advanced engineering. Researchers are working on building robots that can mimic human movements, such as soft robots that are inspired by the way our muscles and bones work. While robots with full muscular-skeletal systems like humans don't yet exist, we are on the verge of creating machines that are more flexible, adaptable, and capable of complex movements. So, is this something we're on track to see soon, or does it belong in the realm of future tech?

3. AI that reads emotions:

Real or Not Real?

Believe it or not, AI that reads emotions is already a part of our lives, although it's not as advanced as you might think. AI systems today can analyze facial expressions, voice tone, and even body language to determine how a person is feeling. This technology is being used in customer service, healthcare, and marketing to better understand human emotions. However, while these AI systems can detect and respond to emotional cues, they do not truly "understand" emotions in the way humans do. They rely on pattern recognition and data, not genuine emotional intelligence. So, is this a technology that's already here, or is it still just an idea for the distant future?

4. AI that develops emotions:

Real or Not Real?

Here's where things get a little more speculative. The concept of AI that develops emotions like Ultron in the Avengers movie remains firmly in the world of fiction. While AI can simulate emotions through programmed responses (such as a chatbot saying it's sorry when it can't help), true emotional development would require AI to experience feelings, which is a far more complex challenge. To create a machine that experiences emotions would require an AI to possess self-awareness and consciousness, concepts that are still deeply debated in philosophy and neuroscience. So, for now, we're still far from achieving AI that can truly feel. Does this belong to science fiction or could it become a reality someday?

Reflect and Engage:

Now that you've had a chance to think through these scenarios, it's time to reflect on the state of artificial intelligence today. As technology continues to advance, the boundaries between what is real and what is possible seem to blur at an ever-accelerating rate. Some of the concepts we once considered impossible are now being actively pursued by researchers and engineers. And as AI continues to evolve, we may soon find ourselves facing questions that challenge our very understanding of humanity and intelligence itself.

We'd love to hear your thoughts! Which of the above scenarios do you think is closest to becoming a reality, and which ones do you think will remain in the realm of fiction for the foreseeable future? Feel free to share your thoughts in the comments section in the Amazon App, and let's continue the conversation about the fascinating world of artificial intelligence.

CHAPTER 9

The Mystery That Powers It All

As we wrap up this journey through the world of artificial intelligence, it's important to take a moment to step back and reflect on something that remains, perhaps, the ultimate mystery: the human brain. Despite all our technological advances, we still don't fully understand how our own minds work. The brain, with its intricate networks of neurons and synapses, continues to astonish scientists and researchers with its complexity. While we have made strides in mapping brain activity and understanding some of its functions, the way thoughts, memories, consciousness, and emotions emerge from the physical structure of the brain is still an enigma. This, in itself, is a paradox. How is it that the most advanced form of intelligence known to us is the very thing we understand the least?

AI, in all its glory, is an attempt to replicate and mimic certain aspects of the brain's functioning. However, no machine, no matter how advanced, has come close to the depth of understanding that the human brain offers. AI can process data, make predictions, and even simulate emotions, but it lacks the fundamental essence that makes humans so uniquely intelligent: the ability to think, reason, and feel on a deeply personal and conscious level. It's easy to get caught up in the marvels of AI and its capacity to outperform humans in specific tasks, but at the heart of it all is a critical truthAI is still just a tool, and it's our brains that give it meaning.

In many ways, AI and the human brain are on parallel paths. Both are systems of immense complexity that work toward achieving specific goals. AI, powered by algorithms and deep learning, is capable of learning from data and improving over time. Similarly, our brains take in information, learn from experience, and adapt. But despite the similarities, the ways in which AI learns are very different from how we, as humans, think and experience the world. AI can simulate intelligence, but it doesn't "experience" it in the way we do. While AI can process information and recognize patterns, it cannot create new ideas in the same organic way our brains do. We may be able to program a machine to "think" in a certain way, but it will never have the lived experience that shapes our own unique intelligence.

This parallel between AI and the human brain should remind us that while artificial intelligence may one day be able to perform tasks better or faster than we can, it still can't replace the nuances and richness of human intelligence. We cannot overlook the fact that AI, for all its promise, is still fundamentally a tool. It's a tool that can assist us, enhance our capabilities, and automate repetitive tasks, but it is not meant to replace us. There is no machine, no program, no algorithm that can replicate the sheer complexity of the human mind. AI is here to assist, to elevate human potential, not to erase it. Our creativity, empathy, and problem-solving abilities are still firmly rooted in the biology of the human brain, and as far as we've come in AI development, that is a fundamental difference that machines cannot overcome.

It's important to keep this in mind as we move forward into a world where AI will play an increasingly prominent role in our daily lives. We may rely on AI to help us with everything from managing our homes to navigating complex business decisions, but it is still humans who will guide these machines, direct their progress, and interpret their results. AI is not here to replace the human element, it's here to amplify it. Our ability to dream, create, and innovate will always be what defines us as a species, and no matter how advanced AI becomes, it will always need a human touch to truly understand the world.

In the grand scheme of things, the relationship between AI and humanity is just beginning. As we continue to push the boundaries of what artificial intelligence can achieve, we should never forget that the brain, the true source of intelligence, remains the most powerful, mysterious, and untapped frontier of all. AI is just one part of the story. The next great adventure in intelligence, both artificial and human, is still unfolding.

Conclusion

Stay Curious, Stay Smart

As we conclude this exploration into the fascinating world of artificial intelligence, one thing is clear: AI is evolving, though often slowly and silently. It doesn't always announce its presence in flashy headlines or bold statements, but behind the scenes, it is quietly reshaping our world in ways we are just beginning to understand. From the smartphones in our pockets to the cars we drive and the systems that govern our societies, AI is already an integral part of our everyday lives, often in ways we don't even notice.

This is why it's so important to stay curious, to keep learning, and to keep observing. AI is not some far-off concept reserved for the pages of science fiction; it is here, right now, and its potential to change the way we live, work, and interact is immense. But as with any powerful tool, understanding it is key. The more we learn about AIthe algorithms that drive it, the ethical implications it presents, and it's true capabilities the better equipped we'll be to make thoughtful, informed decisions about how we use it in our lives. It's not just about understanding the machines themselves but also about understanding the human role in shaping their future.

As AI continues to evolve, so too must our thinking about it. The questions we raise today will be the foundation for the answers of tomorrow. Will AI become more capable of understanding us? Will it ever match or exceed human intelligence? What role will we play as AI becomes more integrated into society? These questions don't have simple answers, but they are important ones, and they require us to stay engaged, to stay smart, and to never stop questioning.

The future of AI is still being written, and it's up to us to help shape it. By staying curious, keeping our minds open, and continuously learning, we can ensure that AI evolves in ways that benefit humanity rather than replacing or undermining what makes us truly human.

So, as you finish this book, remember that the journey doesn't end here. It's only just beginning. Keep watching, keep questioning, and keep learning, because in the world of AI, the more we understand today, the better prepared we'll be for the world we'll live in tomorrow.